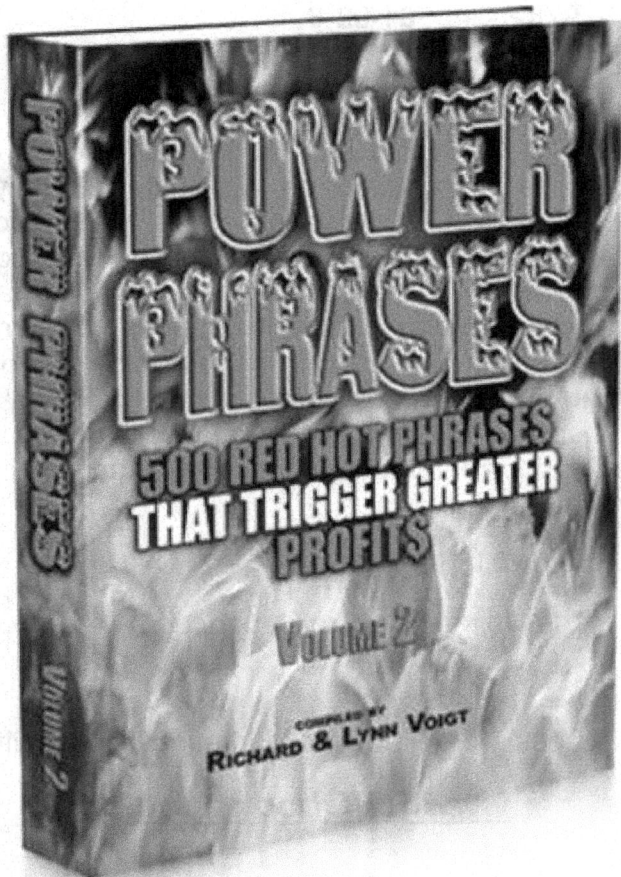

POWER PHRASES – Vol. 2
500 Power Phrases That Trigger Greater Profits

ISBN-13: 978-1-940961-02-6
ISBN-10: 1940961025

First Printing, 2013

Printed in the United States of America

To Access More Powerful Marketing Tools Visit:

www.RIVObooks.com

www.RIVOinc.com

www.WisconsinGarden.com

POWER
PHRASES

Volume 2

500 POWER PHRASES THAT
TRIGGER GREATER
PROFITS

-:|:-•:.*'"''*:•.-:|:-•**•-:|:-•:.*'''''*:•-:|:-

Compiled by
Richard & Lynn Voigt
I.M. Education Specialists

Introduction:

Powerful Phrases, Headlines, Sub Headlines, Slogans, Bullet Points and Interview Sound Bites are perhaps the most powerful marketing tools mankind has ever created. They are the lifeblood behind every business venture are the ultimate secret weapon of Millionaire Marketers.

No matter whether you are introducing or promoting a brand new product, teaching a "How To" skill, building a website, or simply sending an email, using the perfect power phrase is crucial to capturing and holding eyeballs and producing greater marketing profits.

In today's world every word you use has measurable impact. Each word can produce emotional psychological buttons that trigger psychological reactions. Successful advertisers understand that using an effective power phrase is a true art form that turns "wants" into instant gratification "needs." Once artfully triggered, any niche market can instantly create more protifable conversions.

Now it's your turn to personalize this incredible collection of 500 Power Phrases in ways that instantly advance your own effective marketing skills as you create new and power phrases, slogans, presentations, bullet points, or interview sound bites that take you to the next level.

Whether starting or running a small business, writing an ad, coming up with a memorable slogan, making a major corporate presentation, bullet points, creating a video, writing a book, searching for the perfect slogan, teaching a lesson or book report, your creative use of these Power Phrases can capture more eyeballs and produce some amazing rewards quickly turning you into a Marketing Genius. Now, it's your turn to make the magic happen!

POWER PHRASES

Volume 2 – 501- 1000

500 Power Phrases That Trigger Greater Profits

Begin Selecting & Customizing Your Perfect Marketing Phrase

501	Look We All Want This
502	Big Publishers Are In Big Trouble
503	Can You Honestly Put This Off Any Longer
504	Education Is Strip Mining The Minds Of Society
505	Power Behind Being Listed Number One
506	Powerful Ways To Reduce Refunds
507	When Knowing Is Obsolete
508	The Beauty Of This Business Is It's Simplicity
509	Current Education Is Inefficient
510	A Lot Of Things That Make You Feel Great
511	Hedging Your Bets
512	Business Proposal
513	Already Pulling In The Big Profits
514	Ask Them For Recommendations
515	Owning The First Google Page - Priceless
516	Kickin' Butt & Takin' Names
517	Who Says You're Wasting Your Time
518	Let It Shine
519	Wisdom Based Upon Damn Good Advice
520	People Find Time For Things They Care About
521	Become A Unique Specimen

598	The Licensing Loop
599	You Can Copy Me
600	We'll Test Your Ads
601	Make Funny Faces For 20 Minutes A Day
602	Road Mapping Your Business
603	Feats Of Productivity
604	Speak With Enthusiasm
605	The Missing Part Of The Equation
606	Don't Put It Off Any Longer
607	You Can Cancel At Any Time
608	Freebies Are A Hard Turn Down
609	Live That Role
610	Up A Creek Without A Paddle
611	More Information Smarter Decisions
612	Getting Started Is As Easy As 1-2-3
613	Save At Least 50-70% Today
614	This May Take Years To Play Out
615	Access Venture Capital Investors For Your Next Launch
616	Potential To Make Millions
617	The World's Biggest Bluff
618	Making Earned Money Online
619	Replace Bad Habits Fast
620	A Marketing Pecking Order
621	Kick Butt Business Ideas
622	That's What Makes Marketing So Great
623	The Fear Of Failure
624	What's In Store For You
625	Let Me Wet Your Whistle
626	Marketing Home Stretch
627	Living Below What You Can Bare
628	If Long Copy Stinks Think Soap
629	In The Ultimate Context This Has Huge Emotional Value
630	When The Options Are Endless
631	Help Me Take Control
632	Creating Camtasia Callouts
633	Try To Work In Isolation
634	Way To Go Broke Online Fast
635	Remember What Turns Prospects Off

674	Tips For An Irresistible Meeting
675	Nothing Will Be Untouched
676	I Had A Similar Experience
677	Looking For The Motherload
678	Free Enticing Offer Avoids Rookie Mistakes
679	Are Your Space Wasting Headlines Saying Nothing
680	Addicted To Shiny Objects
681	Monday Mayhem Mayday
682	What's The Fix
683	This Will Be Unlike Anything You've Ever Imagined
684	One Simple Change
685	This Is Your Homework For The Next 30-Days
686	More Money More Prosperity
687	Moments Of Glory
688	Monday Morning Marketing
689	Crank Out Winner After Winner
690	Getting The Nod From Sales And Marketing
691	This Is Nuts
692	Savvy Business Plan
693	How People Screw This Up All The Time
694	Hunt Down And Choose Just The "Right" Products
695	Remain Up To Date
696	Some See How The Big Boys Do It
697	Don't Mess With Another Man's Work
698	Forced Into Hiding
699	Simplicity Is The Key To Online Success
700	Why The Main Guys Won't Really Help
701	Avoid Resources That Drain Your Profits
702	Something Is Terribly Wrong
703	Hundreds Of Website Owners Are Signing Up
704	Why Stumble Through Trial And Error
705	Now Is The Time To Act
706	Look For Recommendations
707	Consider Format And Purpose
708	Money Saving Tips
709	The Nature And Nuance Of The Marketing Arc
710	Giveaway Rights
711	Pocket Commissions The Easy Way

712	Ask It In A Different Way
713	Make Your Headlines Appear Important
714	The Exact Opposite Of What They Teach
715	Limited To The Next 500 People
716	June Commission Payment
717	Failure vs. Validate
718	Life Changing Success
719	What Happened Next Was Amazing
720	Instant Classic With A Dash Of Contemporary
721	Want The Motherload Of Traffic
722	Err On The Side Of Doing Too Much
723	Building Online Businesses That Will Beat Any Economic Recession
724	A Simple Plan That Works
725	A Talented Pig Solves A Complex Marketing Problem With Ease
726	How To Land Many Loyal Customers
727	We Like To Keep It Low Key
728	Not Sure What To Say
729	High Flier
730	Even Legends Need A New Look
731	Lowest Payments Ever
732	Article Marketing Strategies In The World Of Web 2.0
733	Crushes Shopping Cart Abandonment
734	Setting Goals And Mission Statements
735	Want A Free Mobile Site
736	This Is Life Changing Information
737	We Are Waiting For You To Join In The Club
738	My Artwork Is Finished
739	Profitable Market Of Very Hungry Subscribers
740	Want To Get Paid Every Day
741	Ways To Sell Your Ad Space Like Crazy
742	Practice But Not Too Much
743	Eligible vs. Ineligible
744	People Will Follow You
745	Seeing Real Growth
746	Keep Changing
747	Largest List Of Big Profits Now Open
748	Push Your Conversions Sky High

786	Are You Willing To Multiple Your Business Every Year
787	Don't Get Lost In Details
788	Embracing A New Mindset
789	I've Always Had BIG Dreams
790	I'm Giving You Another Incredible Option
791	Here's The Short Version
792	Sell Premium Products & Services
793	Start By Scribbling Something
794	Don't Wait Too Long Because This Will Be CLOSING SOON
795	Once The Buzz Gets Going It's Doesn't Stop
796	Why They Will Never Beat This Price
797	Hire The Best For The Lowest Price
798	Spring Into Wisconsin
799	Perfect For Beginners
800	I Just Found These Amazing Training Tools
801	Transform Your Best Features
802	Invest In This Incredible Package
803	Look At All These Great Features
804	Take Everything You've Learned And Apply It To Their Needs
805	Bring Empathy And Caring
806	In Business And Lost It All
807	Light Your Marketing Fire
808	What An Eye Opener
809	Did He Just Go Overboard
810	No Frustrations
811	Sizzling Spring Sale
812	Don't Rationalize Make Excuses Or Point Fingers
813	There Really Is No Free Traffic
814	System Does All The Hard Work
815	Have A Website You Want To Accelerate
816	Video Setup Free Website
817	How Mid And Back List Authors Succeed
818	More Resources Than You'll Ever Need
819	Potential For Rebirth
820	This Is Better Than Posting A Job
821	The Internet Can Be A Scary Place Unless
822	Learn The Story At A Glance
823	Two Hours Of Marketing Is Nothing

14

824	Time To Start Cutting Costs
825	Money Pours Into Businesses Set On Autopilot
826	A Special Deal Just For You
827	Questions Are Our Pattern Of Language
828	Stand Out Better
829	Success In The Shortest Time Available
830	You Don't Need To Go Door To Door
831	Get Into Your Body
832	Hottest Topic For Discussion
833	Target The Right People
834	Make It Easier
835	Condition Yourself For Hope
836	Know The Secret
837	Add Some Value To Life
838	Generous Offer Won't Last Forever
839	Yours Totally Free
840	Most Basic Wealth Principle
841	Everyone With A Computer Is Trying
842	Boring But Useful Information
843	Come Across More Natural
844	How Serious Are You About Your Business
845	Destined To Change Our Industry
846	Entrepreneurs vs. Revolutionaries
847	Blotting Sheets And Face Powder
848	Sure You Can
849	This Is Where A Buyer Is
850	Lack Of Corporate Loyalty Requires A Backup Plan
851	Never Buy This
852	Whine Flu
853	Why 99.5% Of All Online Offers Aren't Being Honest
854	Making Marketing Information Easy To Digest
855	Pretty Toys At Any Price
856	Access Our Crystal Ball
857	Catching Up With An Old Friend
858	No Start Up Costs
859	The Secret Of Building A Great Team
860	Speak With Flowing Breath
861	Lift Your Finger Off The Order Button

862	Find Existing Continuity Offers
863	Learning The Hard Way
864	Place Your Free Ad On Our Ad Board
865	Niches Are Investments
866	It Must Require Less Than 1 Hour Of Your Time
867	Generating Bad Publicity
868	Not Too Big Or Too Small
869	The Main Cash Components Of Your Membership
870	Forget Waiting Months
871	Hope For Incredible Stupidity
872	Create Something Different
873	Health Wealth And Happiness Is Now Available
874	Finding Value To This Process
875	Everyone Is Ready To View Them
876	Congratulations You've Just Made Another Sale
877	Requires Little Editing
878	Grab Your Free Videos Now
879	Create A Happy Relationship With Your Money
880	RE: Account Closure
881	What's The Real Price You're Paying For Procrastination
882	Saving Time And Money
883	What Should I Wear
884	Remember When A Millionaire Use To Get Your Attention
885	It Shadowed My Every Waking Moment
886	Who Are You And Why Should I Listen
887	Nothing Like It Out There
888	Global Guidepost
889	Together We All Achieve More
890	Minimize Multitasking
891	Pouncing On Juicy Headlines
892	Maybe It's All The Craziness
893	Stop Paying Others To Install Your Scripts
894	Pick Up The Essentials
895	You Can See The Results Immediately
896	I've Got A Lot To Tell You About
897	A $100 Billion Dollar Industry And Growing In Any Economy
898	The Most Amazing Thing Of All
899	People Will Buy

900	Never Give Anything Away For Free
901	Never Be Disheartened
902	Generational Difference
903	This Is So Cool
904	Local Or Global Distribution
905	Bills Are Really Annoying Unless
906	I Report You Decide
907	What If The Lottery Came With A Guarantee
908	Start Writing Honest Reviews
909	Making Money Is Easy Keeping It Is Challenging
910	Intuition Says That There's Is Another Way
911	Avoid Hodgepodge Marketing
912	Opportunities Are In The Bag
913	Want To Change The World
914	Creating A New Reality
915	Simply Piece It Together Like A Puzzle
916	Getting A Bad Rap
917	The Most Advanced Technology On The Web
918	Recruit With Words
919	Can And Will Change Your Life
920	Bigger Than The Internet
921	Simple Changes That Make A Huge Difference
922	Here's A Plan For Success
923	Catching Errors
924	The Actual Performance
925	Increasing Everyday
926	Strategic Leverage Provides The Answers
927	What Happens When You Purposely Don't Mention Price
928	Not Just Instant Profit
929	Stable Income From Your Computer
930	Why It's All So Fuzzy
931	Think Like A Marketer
932	Want A Larger Canvas Print
933	What Wisdom Can You Impart
934	Content Management Is Useless Without A Broad Forum
935	Are You Just Spinning Your Wheels Day After Day
936	Affiliate Marketing For Insiders
937	Stop Thinking About It And Act Now

975	The Answer Came To Me
976	Move Into The Happy Customer Arena
977	One Last Closing Thought
978	Appealing To The Millennial Generation
979	Why Am I Doing This
980	Not Naturally Gifted
981	Warm Up Your Voice And Body
982	Don't Be Burdened
983	Market Over A Period Of Time
984	Myth-Buster Tears You Apart
985	Everything You Need Is Set Up And Ready To Go
986	Everyone Will Be Rewarded
987	I'm Being Dead Serious
988	I Know Why You're Here
989	Won't Take Up Extra Time
990	Worried About Your Future
991	How To Handle Lost Sales
992	Six Pack vs. The Keg
993	My Business Made Me Rich
994	Silence The Naysayer Within
995	Dress In A Way That Is Authentic
996	Finding Something You Can Look Forward To
997	Never Cold Call Again
998	Kick Your Salesmanship
999	Don't Settle For Traffic Scraps
1000	Tracking Visitor Intelligence

Lynn and I hope that this "Think Tank" volume series of 500 Hot Phrases will helped you clearly paint your dreams, sell your ideas, and market your messages, propelling each of your ideas and projects toward incredible success. Watch for our next Volume!

We truly wish you the very best and look forward to hearing your success stories.

Concluding Thoughts:

Ever success is built upon a preparing a strong foundation, having a clear vision, and taking positive action each and every day. If you've been searching for a new lifestyle, then you'll find this book directive and inspirational. You can open it to any page and let that page help you rethink possibilities, consider new ideas, open new opportunities, and ultimately experience a more successful and fulfilling lifestyle.

Every problem has a solution! Regardless of your current situation or circumstance, know that you have the power and responsibility to redirect your life in any direction you choose. Simply start thinking about and research the kind of lifestyle that truly appeals to your heart. Begin your new journey by learning everything you can about your chosen subject. When you make that commitment, you'll open more unexpected doors to unique opportunities than imagined.

> **"Creative Thought Is The Only Reality**
> **Everything Else Is Merely The By-Product Of That Thought."**
> - Walter Russell

So why not start thinking **BIGGER? It won't cost you any more.** It all starts by never allowing your current life's situation, environment, or so-called friends to limit your path to a happier, healthier, and successful life. After all, whose life is this?

Make a decision to focus on learning something new each and every day. Begin attracting your ideal lifestyle by doing something you love and enjoy. As difficult as it may be, don't allow money to limit your dreams. Focus on the kind of thoughts that make you feel good. Once you learn how to control your focus, you'll have a great chance to see your dreams take shape. You've finally learn to harness the power you always had within, a Universal Energy stream that flows 365/24/7 in any direction your project your thoughts, Good or Bad. Want proof? The thoughts you currently believe and project reflect the life you're currently living. Therefore, if your life isn't happening, change your thoughts, and change your life. It's something only you can hold, visualize, and project, living your dream come true.

Find yourself a mentor and spend more time with people who truly appreciate, support, and foster your dreams. Life may be short, but the thoughts we hold can make our life wider and more fulfilling.

20

About The Authors:

Richard and Lynn develop creative strategies that paint dreams, sell ideas, & market messages   Together, they present a unique team-approach, working side-by-side, helping clients pursue their passions while sharing their skills and diverse expertise as authors, artists, inventors, entrepreneurs, & Internet marketing education specialists.

Teaching by example, they mentor proven self-publishing services, graphic design, video production, domain acquisition, and marketing research of behalf of their company, RIVO Inc – RIVO Marketing, since 1997. They've created & produced hundreds of videos, self-published dozens of books on a wide variety of topics and created thousands of original works of fine art, while refining their Internet Marketing techniques, mentoring programs, and related business website development.

Their mission is to continually uncover new products and services, test new strategies, and network useful solutions with off and online entrepreneurs, small business owners, writers, local artists, models, teachers, students, and marketing professionals.

Their goal is to help clients create an action plan that discovers and connects the missing pieces of the success puzzle. The goals they foster create multiple streams of income for today's volatile economic climate. Their motto is: "Do the work once and allow the work to create additional streams of income for a lifetime."

Feel free to contact them if you have questions or would like to tap into their talents and expertise. They appreciate your feedback and look forward to hearing your success stories.

Contact:
Richard & Lynn Voigt - RIVO
I. M. Education Specialists

RIVO INC - RIVO Marketing
13720 West Keefe Avenue
Brookfield, Wisconsin 53005 – USA
Email: support@RIVOinc.com
Website: www.RIVObooks.com
Website: www.WisconsinGarden.com

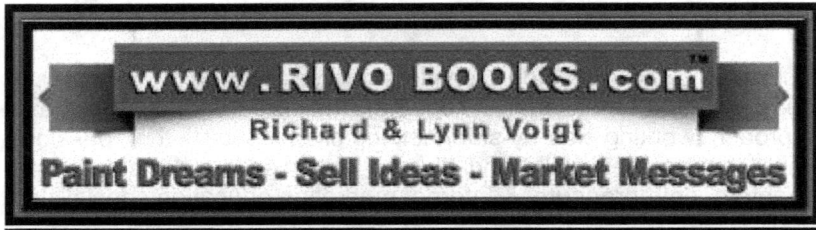

Visit Lynn's Garden: www.WisconsinGarden.com
view hundreds of great garden video blogs Tips

See Richard's Unique Artwork: www.RIVOart.com
view over 3,000 original Fine-Art compositions

Our Book Titles Now Available On Amazon:

THE GOLDEN VAULT OF MOTIVATIONAL QUOTATIONS
Words of Wisdom from The Greatest Minds & Leaders

BABY NAME .ME - 21,400 Names & Nicknames
For Family, Friends, Pets, Natural & Man-Objects

DOODLE DESIGNS Volumes 1-3
For Professionals & Kids Of All Ages
DOODLE DESIGNS – Vol. 1
DOODLE DESIGNS – Vol. 2
DOODLE DESIGNS Coloring Book Vol. 3

Work MORE Accomplish LESS Get FIRED!

ACTION HEADLINES That Drive Emotions – Volumes 1- 6
Paint Dreams, Sell Ideas & Market Your Message
Action Headlines That Drive Emotions Vol. 1
Action Headlines That Drive Emotions Vol. 2
Action Headlines That Drive Emotions Vol. 3
Action Headlines That Drive Emotions Vol. 4
Action Headlines That Drive Emotions Vol. 5
Action Headlines That Drive Emotions Vol. 6

IDIOMS – IDIOMS - IDIOMS
6,450 Popular Expressions That Put Words In Your Mouth

The CLICHÉ BIBLE - 8,400 Clichés For Sports Fanatics
& Lovers Of Popular Expressions

MORE THAN WORDS
5000+ Marketing Phrases That Sell

HYPNOTIC PHRASING
WARNING-This Book Teaches You How To Grab Eyeballs

YOUR RIGHT TO WEALTH
Becoming Wealthy Isn't Hard When You Know How

WI GARDEN – Let's Get Dirty
Our Wisconsin Garden Guide Promoting Delicious, Healthier Home-Grown Fresh Food, With Tools, Tips, & Ideas That Inspire Gardeners!

MONETIZE YOUR SOCIAL LIFE
Earn Extra Income While Having Fun Online

BABY NAMES
21,400 Unique Baby Names & Nicknames

FUNNY HEADLINES vol. 1
3,500 Outrageous Silly Brain Toots

FUNNY HEADLINES vol. 2
3,500 Outrageous Silly Brain Toots

JOBS
10,240 Career Paths That Can Change Your Life!

MONEY WORDS
Powerful Phrases That Million Dollar Copywriters Use To Make Piles Of Cash On Demand!

GARDEN QUOTATIONS
400 Garden Quotes From The Earth To Your Soul

HEADLINE STARTERS
175,000 Words That Paint Dreams, Sell Ideas, And Market Your Message

BABY NAMES
25,350 Baby Names & Nicknames For Your Family Friends & Pets
    697 pages 7,000 Names with Origin & Meaning plus Top 100 Names, And 2,000 Most Popular Names

CURIOUS WORDS
15,800 Words That Expand Your Mind And Change Your Life

INSPIRING THOUGHTS
That Inspire Happiness, Success & A Clearer Understanding Of Life

MARKETING EYEBALLS
100 Ideas That Can Add Unlimited Subscribers To Your Lists

SECOND OF FIVE
My Early Years- From Birth To High School

POWER PHRASES – Individual Volumes 1 - 10
500 Power Phrases That Trigger Greater Profits

POWER PHRASES Pro Edition – Volumes 1-10 (Complete Series)
5000 Power Phrases That Trigger Greater Profits

COMING SOON! – BE THE FIRST TO GRAB YOUR PRO COPY

POWER PHRASES Pro Edition Volumes 1-10 (Complete Series)
5000 Power Phrases That Trigger Greater Profits

What do Marketing Millionaires know that you don't? They know how to pull money out of thin air by using their secret language of Power Phrases.

This Pro Edition of 5000 Red Hot Power Phrases not only saves you time and money but will help jump-start your creative brain in ways you may have never considered. Simply open this amazing collection to any page and find your perfect power phrase. All it may take is simply adding or replacing ONE word. It's simple, quick, and easy!

1. **Want to create more powerful profitable campaign offers?**
2. **Thinking of revitalizing a more professional business identity?**
3. **Want to update old product or service media advertisements?**
4. **Searching for fresh ideas that could improve sales and profits?**
5. **Looking for brand new ways to create stronger media sales copy?**
6. **Ready to use millionaire strategies advancing you to the next level?**

5000 POWER PHRASES is exclusively for professional Internet Marketers, authors,advertisers, executives, business owners, TV & radio reporters, entrepreneurs, administrators, managers, supervisors, teachers and students who want to find and access unique phrases for marketing slogans, presentation bullet points, and interview sound bites that powerfully paint dreams, sell ideas, and market your message.

Stop wasting valuable time, money, and energy racking your brain for new ideas. Create more profitable power phrase marketing campaigns for all your products, services, slogans, bullet points, and interview sound bites that finally grab and hold people's attention and trigger greater profits?

You now have a very powerful and professional marketing tool in your hand. We are confident that you know how to use it wisely in order to maximize the potential of all your marketing campaigns! Lynn and I **Thank You** for your support and purchase.

CLAIM 500 MORE POWER PHRASES!

Thank you for purchasing this eBook and in doing so we would like to send you **500 More Red Hot Power Phrases for FREE!**

When you post a **positive review of this Book on Amazon Books** under this title you'll receive an additional **500 POWER PHRASES**. Your review may also be sent directly to us.

Your request must be received within 30-days of purchase. Once your positive Book review is posted and verified, simply email the following to **(500@RIVOinc.com)**:

1. Full Name of Purchaser
2. Email address
3. Paypal Invoice Number
4. Copy of your posted Book Review*

Once we receive the above, we'll send you 500 Power Phrases **(PDF)** emailed to the address you provided.

Visit: www.RIVObooks.com for additional volumes as they become available including the Pro Edition of 5000 Red Hot Power Phrases that say what you mean to say and trigger greater profits.

Lynn and I look forward to your written comments and suggestions as we love hearing from each of our readers.

Richard & Lynn Voigt
RIVO Inc – RIVO Marketing
13720 West Keefe Avenue
Brookfield, Wisconsin 53005 USA
Telephone: (262) 783-5335
www.RIVObooks.com

P. S. If you love gardening, catch us on www.WisconsinGarden.com

*NOTE: This offer is valid providing it does not violate the terms of service of the entity with whom you made this purchase. Duplicate or incomplete entries will also not be eligible and this offer is limited to one request per email address. All eligible review submissions become the property of RIVO Inc - RIVO Marketing – RIVO books and may be used as promotional testimonials ads on RIVO Inc websites. This offer may be withdrawn at any time without prior written notice.

www.ingramcontent.com/pod-product-compliance
Lightning Source LLC
Chambersburg PA
CBHW060709280326
41933CB00012B/2361